SPONSORSHIP PAGE

THIS BOOK IS SPONSORED BY

....

....

AS A GIFT TO

....

....

ON THIS DAY

....

'Each one must give as he has decided in his heart,
not reluctantly or under compulsion,
for God loves a cheerful giver.'
(2 Corinthians 9:7, ESV)

BY PRAYER M. MADUEKE

PRAYERS FOR PREGNANT WOMEN

BOOK 15 OF 40 PRAYER GIANTS

FREE EBOOKS

In order to say a 'Thank You' for purchasing *Prayers for Pregnant Women*, I offer these books to you in appreciation.

> **Click here or go to madueke.com/free-gift to download the eBooks now** <

MESSAGE FROM THE AUTHOR

PRAYER M. MADUEKE
CHRISTIAN AUTHOR

My name is Prayer Madueke, a spiritual warrior in the Lord's vineyard, an accomplished author, speaker, and expert on spiritual warfare and deliverance. I have published well over 100 books on every area of successful Christian living. I am an acclaimed family and relationship counselor with several titles dealing with critical areas in the lives of the children of God. I travel to several countries each year speaking and conducting deliverance sessions, breaking the yokes of demonic oppression and setting captives free.

It would be a delight to collaborate with you or your ministry in organized crusades, ceremonies, marriages and marriage seminars, special events, church ministration and fellowship for the advancement of God's kingdom here on earth.

You can find all my books on my website: madueke.com.

They have produced many testimonies and I want your testimony to be one too. God bless you.

CHRISTIAN COUNSELLING

We were created for a greater purpose than only survival and God wants us to live a full life.

If you need prayer or counselling, or if you have any other inquiries, please visit the counselling page on my website madueke.com/counselling to know when I will be available for a phone call.

EMAIL NEWSLETTER & ANNOUNCEMENTS

Never miss a message from me again! People who read my newsletters say that they have been one of the most important tools in their Christian walk. The best part is that a subscription is, and always will be, completely free. As a subscriber on my mailing list, you'll be the first to hear about my new book releases, be invited to my weekly prayer sessions, and get reminders about my blog posts and other helpful information.

To subscribe, please visit the newsletter page on my website madueke.com/newsletter.

DEDICATION

This book is dedicated to pregnant women who are trusting God to deliver their children safely. The Lord who sees your sincere dedication will answer your prayers Amen.

TABLE OF CONTENTS

ONE

THE WEAKER VESSEL

A woman's softness and tenderness depicts her as the weaker vessel. A woman is not tough like a man is. Therefore, she requires prayers and encouragement, especially during pregnancy. You must not be negative and rigid against your wife during her pregnancy. However, these weak attributes should not influence a woman's relationship with God or character negatively. If a pregnant woman dies in her pregnancy as a sinner, she would definitely go to hell fire. Therefore, as a pregnant woman, you should maintain your relationship with God, with your husband and others.

Who can find a virtuous woman? For her price is far above rubies. The heart of her husband doth safely trust in her, so that he shall have no need of spoil. She will do him good and not evil all the days of her life. She seeketh wool, and flax, and worketh willingly with her hands. She is like the merchants' ships; she bringeth her food from afar

— PROVERBS 31:10-14

Virtue is one word for the excellent qualities, the desirable personality traits and the endearing comportment in character, which every man longs for in his wife. A virtuous woman's price is far above rubies and she is the joy of her husband. In times of pregnancy, the weakness of the woman should not affect her character and relationship with others.

TWO

QUALITIES OF A VIRTUOUS WIFE

A virtuous wife does everything possible to preserve her respect and trust for her husband at all times. Even during her pregnancy, she endeavors to be good to her husband and her household. A virtuous woman can go the extra mile to retain her honor and build her house. She is stable in character. A virtuous woman possesses enviable qualities and lives an industrious life. She is resourceful, liberal and submissive. She inspires confidence in her husband's life. The bible honored virtuous women severally.

A gracious woman retaineth honor: and strong
men retain riches

— PROVERBS 11:16

A virtuous woman is a crown to her husband:
but she that maketh ashamed is as rottenness
in his bones

— PROVERBS 12:4

Every wise woman buildeth her house: but the foolish plucketh it down with her hands

— PROVERBS 14:1

No matter how weak her body is, she remains strong in character and never loses her respect no matter what.

[15]She riseth also while it is yet night, and giveth meat to her household, and a portion to her maidens. [16]She considereth a field, and buyeth it: with the fruit of her hands, she planteth a vineyard. [17]She girdeth her loins with strength, and strengtheneth her arms. [18]She perceiveth that her merchandise is good: her candle goeth not out by night. [19]She layeth her hands to the spindle, and her hands hold the distaff. [22]She maketh herself coverings of tapestry; her clothing is silk and purple

— PROVERBS 31:15-19, 22

Even during her pregnancy, she maintains her life of industry and kindness. She may not participate fully during pregnancy, but she plans her timetable and gives instructions with respect and wisdom.

SHE MAINTAINS HER DISCRETION

Discretion is very important to every virtuous woman. They want to maintain good judgment at all times at their homes. She cares for all persons under her control and supervision. She is a good planner, a sustainer of good behavior and knows how to approach matters carefully. She knows the cost of foolishness.

As a jewel of gold in a swine's snout, so is a fair woman which is without discretion

— PROVERBS 11:22

And Nabal answered David's servants, and said, Who is David? And who is the son of Jesse? There be many servants now a days that break away every man from his master. Shall I then take my bread, and my water, and my flesh that I have killed for my shearers, and give it unto men, whom I know not whence they be? So David's young men turned their way, and went again, and came and told him all those sayings. And David said unto his men, Gird ye on every man his sword. And they girded on every man his sword; and David also girded on his sword:

and there went up after David about four
hundred men; and two hundred abode by the
stuff

— 1 SAMUEL 25:10-13

Her wisdom moves her into action at the right time. A virtuous
woman is determined to obey her husband, submit to him and
play her own part well. No matter how wicked her husband may
be, she tries to satisfy him in order to obey God's Word.

18Then Abigail made haste, and took two
hundred loaves, and two bottles of wine, and
five sheep ready dressed, and five measures of
parched corn, and an hundred clusters of
raisins, and two hundred cakes of figs, and laid
them on asses. 19And she said unto her servants,
Go on before me; behold, I come after you. But
she told not her husband Nabal. 20And it was so,
as she rode on the ass, that she came down by
the covert of the hill, and, behold, David and his
men came down against her; and she met them.
23And when Abigail saw David, she hasted, and
lighted off the ass, and fell before David on her
face, and bowed herself to the ground, 24And

fell at his feet, and said, Upon me, my lord, upon me let this iniquity be: and let thine handmaid, I pray thee, speak in thine audience, and hear the words of thine handmaid. [25]Let not my lord, I pray thee, regard this man of Belial, even Nabal: for as his name is, so is he; Nabal is his name, and folly is with him: but I thine handmaid saw not the young men of my lord, whom thou didst send. [26]Now therefore, my lord, as the LORD liveth, and as thy soul liveth, seeing the LORD hath withholden thee from coming to shed blood, and from avenging thyself with thine own hand, now let thine enemies, and they that seek evil to my lord, be as Nabal. [27]And now this blessing which thine handmaid hath brought unto my lord, let it even be given unto the young men that follow my lord. [35]So David received of her hand that which she had brought him, and said unto her, Go up in peace to thine house; see, I have hearkened to thy voice, and have accepted thy person

— 1 SAMUEL 25:18-20, 23-27, 35

Her godly character and behavior can challenge the worst man on earth to change his mind to do well instead of evil.

Discretion has to do with wisdom in conduct and the tactful handling of difficult situations. A virtuous woman knows that her chief calling is to take care of her home.

> And she said, Truth, Lord: yet the dogs eat of the crumbs which fall from their masters' table. Then Jesus answered and said unto her, O woman, great is thy faith: be it unto thee even as thou wilt. And her daughter was made whole from that very hour
>
> — MATTHEW 15:27-28

A virtuous wife knows how to cry to God or prays extensively in order to save every soul under her care. The woman of Canaan came out of the coast all the way to cry unto Jesus. She prayed until Jesus had mercy on her daughter. Virtuous women concentrate their energy working hard to make everyone at their homes happy.

They are excellent in home management. They are not wasteful, quarrelsome or rude in character. They are prayerful and careful in making choices.

That they may teach the young women to be
sober, to love their husbands, to love their
children, To be discreet, chaste, keepers at
home, good, obedient to their own husbands,
that the word of God be not blasphemed

— TITUS 2:4-5

Her positive lifestyle influences everyone in her house to behave well, be sober and respectful.

SHE IS DILIGENT

A virtuous wife helps the less privileged people and gives gifts to the needy at every given opportunity. She is known for her kindness. She can take risks to see that the people around her are happy. Like Jesus, she has a deep love for compassion and seeing people set free from bondage. A virtuous woman is ready to do anything to help people get well and serve God. She understands that time is too short and that eternity is endless. That is why she is always willing to see people liberated from sin, sickness and death. No trouble is so great for her to handle.

[20]She stretcheth out her hand to the poor; yea,
she reacheth forth her hands to the

needy. [24]She maketh fine linen, and selleth it; and delivereth girdles unto the merchant. [27]She looketh well to the ways of her household, and eateth not the bread of idleness

— PROVERBS 31:20, 24, 27

There is no humiliation to deep, no labor to hard, and no love too strong in her efforts to save souls from trouble. A virtuous woman is a great overseer with wisdom in administration at the home front. At home, she is involved. She does not enjoy relaxing and issuing orders. Instead, she engages in the daily assignments at her home and offices where she is in-charge.

Whatsoever thy hand findeth to do, do it with thy might; for there is no work, nor device, nor knowledge, nor wisdom, in the grave, whither thou goest

— ECCLESIASTES 9:10

Now there was at Joppa a certain disciple named Tabitha, which by interpretation is called Dorcas: this woman was full of good works and alms deeds which she did. Then Peter arose and

went with them. When he was come, they
brought him into the upper chamber: and all the
widows stood by him weeping, and shewing the
coats and garments which Dorcas made, while
she was with them

— ACTS 9:36, 39

A virtuous woman is not lazy or wicked. She works with all her
might, a willing heart and divine wisdom. She is full of good
works and deeds. She wins many souls for God. Her
distinctions cannot be hidden.

Strength and honor are her clothing; and she
shall rejoice in time to come. She openeth her
mouth with wisdom; and in her tongue is the
law of kindness. [28]Her children arise up, and call
her blessed; her husband also, and he praiseth
her. Many daughters have done virtuously, but
thou excellest them all. Favor is deceitful, and
beauty is vain: but a woman that feareth the
LORD, she shall be praised. Give her of the fruit
of her hands; and let her own works praise her
in the gates

— PROVERBS 31:25-26, 28-31

Virtuous women work with eternity in view and do not procrastinate. They are always with honor and are usually very kind. They are very spiritual and they control their tongues very well. They are the perfect models to follow because they fear God. They are filled with honest reports.

And in the sixth month the angel Gabriel was sent from God unto a city of Galilee, named Nazareth, To a virgin espoused to a man whose name was Joseph, of the house of David; and the virgin's name was Mary. And the angel came in unto her, and said, Hail, thou that art highly favored, the Lord is with thee: blessed art thou among women

— LUKE 1:26-28

In like manner also, that women adorn themselves in modest apparel, with shamefacedness and sobriety; not with broided hair, or gold, or pearls, or costly array; But (which becometh women professing godliness) with good works

— 1 TIMOTHY 2:9-10

The beauty of a virtuous wife resonates in her character. Her children, husband and family members respect and praise her. Her works are rooted in God and she is special among women.

> Likewise, ye wives, be in subjection to your own husbands; that, if any obey not the word, they also may without the word be won by the conversation of the wives; While they behold your chaste conversation coupled with fear. Whose adorning let it not be that outward adorning of plaiting the hair, and of wearing of gold, or of putting on of apparel; But let it be the hidden man of the heart, in that which is not corruptible, even the ornament of a meek and quiet spirit, which is in the sight of God of great price. For after this manner in the old time the holy women also, who trusted in God, adorned themselves, being in subjection unto their own husbands
>
> — 1 PETER 3:1-5

She is submissive, obedient and a specialists in approaching matters prudently. She tries to excel in every good thing in life.

She is always distinguishable, outshining and first rated above others. Virtuous women try their best to be outstanding, exceptional, superior and best of the best.

SHE SUBMITS TO HER HUSBAND

One of the qualities of a virtuous woman is submission to the authority of her husband even during pregnancy. A virtuous woman recognizes and accepts God's ordained headship of her husband. This she does, not because her husband is fulfilling his own part in the marriage but because she wants to obey God's Word as a Christian. The Word of God guides her:

> Likewise, ye wives, be in subjection to your own husbands; that, if any obey not the word, they also may without the word be won by the conversation of the wives
>
> — 1 PETER 3:1

> Wives, submit yourselves unto your own husbands, as it is fit in the Lord
>
> — COLOSSIANS 3:18

A Christian wife has nothing to lose in submitting to the headship of her husband. By doing so, she receives the blessing of obeying God's Word.

"Wives, submit yourselves unto your own husbands, as unto the Lord. [24]Therefore as the church is subject unto Christ, so let the wives be to their own husbands in everything

— EPHESIANS 5:22, 24

Submitting as "unto the Lord" means that the wife is to submit in love, not as slaves who fearfully obey. Virtuous women manifest the quality of being meek and quiet to the glory of God.

On the seventh day, when the heart of the king was merry with wine, he commanded Mehuman, Biztha, Harbona, Bigtha, and Abagtha, Zethar, and Carcas, the seven chamberlains that served in the presence of Ahasuerus the king, To bring Vashti the queen before the king with the crown royal, to shew the people and the princes her beauty: for she was fair to look on. But the queen Vashti refused to come at the king's commandment by his chamberlains: therefore was the king very wroth, and his anger burned in him

— ESTHER 1: 10-12

Consider Esther, who was so quiet, meek and gentle. She was also hospitable, loving and humble.

And it fell on a day, that Elisha passed to Shunem, where was a great woman; and she constrained him to eat bread. And so it was, that as oft as he passed by, he turned in thither to eat bread. And she said unto her husband, Behold now, I perceive that this is a holy man of God, which passeth by us continually. Let us make a little chamber, I pray thee, on the wall; and let us set for him there a bed, and a table, and a stool, and a candlestick: and it shall be, when he cometh to us that he shall turn in thither. And it fell on a day, that he came thither, and he turned into the chamber, and lay there. And he said to Gehazi his servant, Call this Shunammite. And when he had called her, she stood before him. And he said unto him, Say now unto her, Behold, thou hast been careful for us with all this care; what is to be done for thee? Wouldest thou be spoken for to the king, or to the captain of the host? And she answered, I dwell among mine own people. And he said, What then is to be done for her? And Gehazi answered, Verily she hath no child, and her husband is old

— 2 KING 4:8-14

A virtuous woman is very conscious and heavenly bound. She is loving and prayerful.

And, behold, a woman of Canaan came out of the same coasts, and cried unto him, saying, Have mercy on me, O Lord, thou Son of David; my daughter is grievously vexed with a devil. But he answered her not a word. And his disciples came and besought him, saying, Send her away; for she crieth after us. But he answered and said, I am not sent but unto the lost sheep of the house of Israel. Then came she and worshipped him, saying, Lord, help me. But he answered and said, It is not meet to take the children's bread, and to cast it to dogs. And she said, Truth, Lord: yet the dogs eat of the crumbs, which fall from their masters' table. Then Jesus answered and said unto her, O woman, great is thy faith: be it unto thee even as thou wilt. And her daughter was made whole from that very hour

— MATTHEW 15: 22-28

They are also humble in character. She makes her home a paradise, conducive for her husband, children and the servants.

THREE

HUSBAND'S CARE DURING PREGNANCY

Every husband has so much to do during the wife's pregnancy. It is the responsibility of a husband to bring out the best in his wife. No matter how much progress a woman has made before marriage, if her husband plays his role very well, the woman will rise to greater positions of excellence.

> For the husband is the head of the wife, even as Christ is the head of the church: and he is the savior of the body
>
> — EPHESIANS 5:23

But I would have you know, that the head of
every man is Christ; and the head of the woman
is the man; and the head of Christ is God

— 1 CORINTHIAN 11:3

One that ruleth well his own house, having his
children in subjection with all gravity; (For if a
man know not how to rule his own house, how
shall he take care of the church of God?)

— 1 TIMOTHY 3:4-5

The husband is the head of the wife and the head of the man is
Christ, while the head of Christ is God. The harmony between
God and Christ dislodged the devil. Jesus was able to do all that
He did because He was one with God.

At that time Jesus answered and said, I thank
thee, O Father, Lord of heaven and earth,
because thou hast hid these things from the
wise and prudent, and hast revealed them unto
babes

— MATTHEW 11:25

And when Jesus had cried with a loud voice, he said, Father, into thy hands I commend my spirit: and having said thus, he gave up the ghost

— LUKE 23:46

I can of mine own self do nothing: as I hear, I judge: and my judgment is just; because I seek not mine own will, but the will of the Father which hath sent me

— JOHN 5:30

A husband and his wife must stay together in order to achieve their aim and purpose of their marriage. Jesus never wanted to be independent of His Father. He was always grateful to His Father. At the cross, He commended His Spirit unto God, His Father and head. He knows that a body without head can do nothing. He depended on His Father to do all things He did on earth. This is how a husband and his wife must depend on each other.

A good husband who understands what a head is to the body cannot plan alone. He must stay with the wife, plan with her spiritually and provide all her earthly needs. As the head, he must plan for the welfare of the whole family including the baby in the womb. This is a God's given responsibility. In order to be a responsible man and a good head, he must plan, teach, guide, direct, lead and control the family according to God's Word. He prays together with his wife and provides for the entire family. The head stays with the body until death.

> [28]So ought men to love their wives as their own bodies. He that loveth his wife loveth himself. [29]For no man ever yet hated his own flesh; but nourisheth and cherisheth it, even as the Lord the church: [31]For this cause shall a man leave his father and mother, and shall be joined unto his wife, and they two shall be one flesh.
>
> — EPHESIANS 5:28- 29, 31

Christ was fully involved with His disciples until the end. Even when they scattered and denied Him, he loved them. He showed His love and died to save the church. Even after death, He rose, gathered them again and empowered them to continue the work of the gospel.

> Afterward he appeared unto the eleven as they sat at meat, and upbraided them with their unbelief and hardness of heart, because they

believed not them which had seen him after he was risen. And he said unto them, Go ye into all the world, and preach the gospel to every creature. He that believeth and is baptized shall be saved; but he that believeth not shall be damned. And these signs shall follow them that believe; In my name shall they cast out devils; they shall speak with new tongues; They shall take up serpents; and if they drink any deadly thing, it shall not hurt them; they shall lay hands on the sick, and they shall recover. So then after the Lord had spoken unto them, he was received up into heaven, and sat on the right hand of God. And they went forth, and preached everywhere, the Lord working with them, and confirming the word with signs following. Amen

— MARK 16:14-20

Christ did not only die for the church, he resurrected and empowered the church. Up until today, he is with the church, working with the church and confirming the Word they speak with signs following. Christ was not just a head to the church, but a good head and not a figurehead. He is still involved in life and functions of the church until this day.

INCREASE OF MAN'S RESPONSIBILITY

Jesus love, care and concern for His bride, the church, increase at our weakest moments. Christ came to save us when it was necessary that His perfect nature of godhead and sinless blood would remove guilt, shame and death from us. His grace appeared at our hopeless and helpless moment. As the scriptures put it:

Your lamb shall be without blemish, a male of the first year: ye shall take it out from the sheep, or from the goats

— EXODUS 12:5

And whosoever offereth a sacrifice of peace offerings unto the LORD to accomplish his vow, or a freewill offering in beeves or sheep, it shall be perfect to be accepted; there shall be no blemish therein

— LEVITICUS 22:21

Giving thanks unto the Father, which hath made us meet to be partakers of the inheritance of the saints in light: Who hath delivered us from the power of darkness, and hath translated us into the kingdom of his dear Son: In whom we have redemption through his blood, even the forgiveness of sins

— COLOSSIANS 1:12-14

We received the grace of Jesus when we were blind, deaf and dead. If Christ did not come to save us, we would be in hell by now. A husband is expected to discharge his God-given role and responsibility over his wife during the time of pregnancy. This is because women are usually weak at this period and needs more help and love.

Husbands, love your wives, even as Christ also loved the church, and gave himself for it; That he might sanctify and cleanse it with the washing of water by the word, That he might present it to himself a glorious church, not having spot, or wrinkle, or any such thing; but that it should be holy and without blemish. So ought men to love their wives as their own

bodies. He that loveth his wife loveth himself.
For no man ever yet hated his own flesh; but
nourisheth and cherisheth it, even as the Lord
the church: For we are members of his body, of
his flesh, and of his bones. For this cause shall a
man leave his father and mother, and shall be
joined unto his wife, and they two shall be one
flesh. This is a great mystery: but I speak
concerning Christ and the church. Nevertheless
let every one of you in particular so love his wife
even as himself; and the wife see that she
reverence her husband

— EPHESIANS 5:25-33

Husbands are expected to take care of their wives just as they do to their own bodies. Every man naturally feeds, protects, washes, cleans and cares for his body. Nobody wishes to cut off his leg because it was dirty, or force his hands to sleep under the rain because they were dirty.

Unfortunately, some unreasonable husbands insist that their wives sweep, wash, cook and do all the works alone even at their ninth month of pregnancy. They cannot allow their wives to rest even when it is clear they are weak and need to rest. Even at their wives' sick beds, they expect them to get up to wash the plates and clean the room.

Such men knew how to sympathize with everybody else except their wives. They know how to take good care of their bodies, rest when they are sick or tired but insist that their wives do not. They grant their bodies rest well but force their wives to wake up early. They cannot tell when their wives are in pain. They increase their wives' sorrows, pains and cause them to get weaker. Ironically, they also claim to be born-again, but beat their wives, abuse them and forbid them from complaining to others. Do you love your wife as Christ loves the church and gave His life for her?

> For when we were yet without strength, in due time Christ died for the ungodly. For scarcely for a righteous man will one die: yet peradventure for a good man some would even dare to die. But God commendeth his love toward us, in that, while we were yet sinners, Christ died for us. Much more then, being now justified by his blood, we shall be saved from wrath through him. For if, when we were enemies, we were reconciled to God by the death of his Son, much more, being reconciled, we shall be saved by his life

— ROMANS 5:6-10

And as they went to tell his disciples, behold, Jesus met them, saying, All hail. And they came and held him by the feet, and worshipped him. Then said Jesus unto them, Be not afraid: go tell my brethren that they go into Galilee, and there shall they see me

— MATTHEW 28:9-10

Imagine how Christ washed the feet of His disciples when they all had the strength to do so. What Christ demonstrated was a remarkable service to one another. He demonstrated the ministry of love, which places the interest of *self* behind and below that of others.

So after He had washed their feet, and had taken his garments, and was set down again, he said unto them, Know ye what I have done to you? Ye call me Master and Lord: and ye say well; for so I am. If I then, your Lord and Master, have washed your feet; ye also ought to wash one another's feet. For I have given you an example that ye should do as I have done to

you. Verily, verily, I say unto you, The servant is
not greater than his lord; neither he that is sent
greater than he that sent him

— JOHN 13: 12-16

For, brethren, ye have been called unto liberty;
only use not liberty for an occasion to the flesh,
but by love serve one another

— GALATIANS 5:13

Bear ye one another's burdens, and so fulfill the
law of Christ. As we have therefore opportunity,
let us do good unto all men, especially unto
them who are of the household of faith

— GALATIANS 6:2, 10

The washing of feet was an oriental custom of great antiquity as
a mark of hospitality. The Scriptures pointed out the
significance of the washing of feet:

Let a little water, I pray you, be fetched, and
wash your feet, and rest yourselves under the
tree

— GENESIS 18: 4

And he said, Behold now, my lords, turn in, I
pray you, into your servant's house, and tarry all
night, and wash your feet, and ye shall rise up
early, and go on your ways. And they said, Nay;
but we will abide in the street all night

— GENESIS 19:2

If you could care for others, Christ demanded that you care more for your wife. Christ did it for us when we could not. For when we were yet without strength, Christ died for the ungodly and unworthy. Loving, caring and cherishing your wife is a commandment, which you must do whether she deserves it or not. It is a command that you must obey and there is blessing in obeying God's Word.

As God showered us with His love without minding that we are not worthy, so shall we do to our wives without minding their failures.

Now before the feast of the Passover, when
Jesus knew that his hour was come that he
should depart out of this world unto the Father,

having loved his own which were in the world,
he loved them unto the end

— JOHN 13:1

Greater love hath no man than this, that a man
lay down his life for his friends

— JOHN 15:13

Do not love only when you are sure of what you can get from your wife. You must establish your love on the written Word of God, which commands you to love. Christ's love for us was sacrificial. Therefore, your love for your wife must be sacrificial before God accepts it.

56But all this was done, that the scriptures of the prophets might be fulfilled. Then all the disciples forsook him, and fled. 66What think ye? They answered and said, He is guilty of death. 67Then did they spit in his face, and buffeted him; and others smote him with the palms of their hands, 68Saying, Prophesy unto us, thou Christ, Who is he that smote thee? 69Now Peter sat without in the palace: and a damsel came unto him, saying, Thou also wast with Jesus of Galilee. ⁷⁰But he denied before them all, saying, I know not what thou sayest. ⁷¹And when he was gone out into the porch, another maid saw him, and said unto them that were there, This fellow was also with Jesus of Nazareth. ⁷²And again he denied with an oath, I do not know the man. ⁷³And after a while came unto him they that stood by, and said to Peter, Surely thou also art one of them; for thy speech bewrayeth thee. ⁷⁴Then began he to curse and to swear, saying, I know not the man. And immediately the cock crew. ⁷⁵And Peter remembered the word of Jesus, which said unto him, Before the cock crow, thou shalt deny me thrice. And he went out, and wept bitterly

— MATTHEW 26: 56, 66-75

Imagine the disciples of Jesus fleeing at the time Jesus needed them most. They arrested Jesus, spit on his face and smote him. Yet, He went ahead and died for our sins. What has your wife or husband done to you that you cannot forgive for Christ's sake?

FOUR

WHAT A HUSBAND AND WIFE MUST DO

The place of love in a Christian home cannot be over emphasized. No husband and wife can fulfill God's purpose in their marriage without practicing the true love. At the presence of true love, a husband and his wife can move mountains. Christ our perfect example demonstrated true love by loving God, His followers and His enemies at all times in a sacrificial manner. What does the Scripture demand from us in reciprocation?

> Hereby perceive we the love of God, because
> he laid down his life for us: and we ought to lay
> down our lives for the brethren

¹Now before the feast of the Passover, when Jesus knew that his hour was come that he should depart out of this world unto the Father, having loved his own which were in the world, he loved them unto the end. ¹³Ye call me Master and Lord: and ye say well; for so I am. ¹⁴If I then, your Lord and Master, have washed your feet; ye also ought to wash one another's feet. ¹⁵For I have given you an example that ye should do as I have done to you

— JOHN 13:1, 13-15

Love demands and should be demonstrated in deed as Christ did. True love when demonstrated gives contentment to live and stay in fellowship.

And when he was come into the ship, he that had been possessed with the devil prayed him that he might be with him

— MARK 5:18

A husband who must love his wife as God demanded must die to self and where this kind of love exists, there is no animosity, struggle, fighting, but a perfect and glorious harmony. The great secret of joy, happiness and peace in marriage is mutual love, tenderness, loveliness and kindness of character at home. God demands that the wife should respect, honor and obey the husband, while the husband should love and care for the wife and direct the affairs of the house.

> Forbearing one another, and forgiving one another, if any man have a quarrel against any: even as Christ forgave you, so also do ye
>
> — COLOSSIANS 3:13

> And be ye kind one to another, tenderhearted, forgiving one another, even as God for Christ's sake hath forgiven you
>
> — EPHESIANS 4:32

Husbands and wives must forgive each other no matter the offence. If they quarrel, they must take decision in advanced to forgive each other. They must not allow bitterness, anger, wrath, clamor, evil speaking or gossip to come between them.

They must be kind, and of tender heart to one another. They are commanded by God's Word to prefer one to another, minister to one another and consider one another.

> Be kindly affectioned one to another with
> brotherly love; in honor preferring one another
>
> — ROMANS 12:10

> And let us consider one another to provoke
> unto love and to good works
>
> — HEBREW 10:24

You must be kindly affected with love to one another, preferring one another in love. You are also commanded to consider one another, provoke one another unto love. The husband should consider his wife by taking over most of her job during her pregnancy. Things like finding faults, hatred, quarrelling, malice, criticism, revenge, bitterness, selfishness, backbiting and unforgiving attitude should not be mentioned or found in your home, especially during your wife's pregnancy.

PRAYERS FOR PREGNANT WOMEN

Bible references: Exodus 23:25-26; Proverbs 31:10-31

Begin with praise and worship

End every step with prayers as you led

STEP 1

Father Lord, arise and protect me from defilement, in the name of Jesus. I receive power to function without satanic attacks, in the name of Jesus. Every weakness that is designed to destroy my divine character, die by fire, in the name of Jesus. O Lord, arise and deliver me from strange weaknesses, in the name of Jesus. Any power that wants to use my pregnancy to ruin my Christian life, die, in the name of Jesus. Let the arrow of death that was fired at me backfire by force, in the name of Jesus. Blood of Jesus, speak life unto my baby in the womb, in the name of Jesus. Every weapon of witchcraft against my pregnancy, catch fire, in the name of Jesus. Holy Ghost fire, saturate my womb and protect my pregnancy, in the name of Jesus. Let my relationship with God and man be preserved within and outside this pregnancy, in the name of Jesus. Any power that wants to attack my virtue during my pregnancy, die, in the name of Jesus. Any satanic door that was opened to this pregnancy, close by force, in the name of Jesus. I reject evil weakness that was designed to abort my pregnancy, in the name of Jesus.

STEP 2

O Lord, empower me to respect my husband throughout my pregnancy period, in the name of Jesus. Let the plans of devil to destroy me with the works of the flesh die, in the name of Jesus. O Lord, empower me to maintain peace and joy during my pregnancy, in the name of Jesus. Let every good thing inside me be sustained during this pregnancy, in the name of Jesus. I refuse to take any negative action during this pregnancy, in the name of Jesus. I frustrate demons of miscarriage in my life, in the name of Jesus. Holy Ghost fire, cover my womb and protect my baby to Your own glory, in the name of Jesus. O Lord, increase my strength during this pregnancy, in the name of Jesus. Let star hijackers of pregnancies be disgraced for my sake, in the name of Jesus. Let evil eyes that are monitoring my pregnancy go blind, in the name of Jesus. I frustrate every manipulation of my pregnancy, in the name of Jesus. Killers of babies in the womb, my pregnancy is not available, in the name of Jesus. Every arrow of death that was fired at my pregnancy, I fire you back, in the name of Jesus. Any evil altar that is attacking my pregnancy, scatter by fire, in the name of Jesus. Blood of Jesus, cleanse every evil mark that is made on my pregnancy, in the name of Jesus.

STEP 3

Any curse that was placed upon my pregnancy, expire by fire, in the name of Jesus. Every unclean spirit that is contending with my pregnancy, I cast you out, in the name of Jesus. I command the destroying fire of God to destroy every enemy of my pregnancy, in the name of Jesus. Every satanic rage against my pregnancy, be calmed, in the name of Jesus. Any power that is oppressing my pregnancy, I oppress you, in the name of Jesus. Any evil brain that is planning to destabilize my pregnancy, scatter, in the name of Jesus. Wherever they mention my pregnancy for evil, blood of Jesus, answer, in the name of Jesus. Let every enemy of my pregnancy receive double destruction, in the name of Jesus. Any poison that is prepared against my pregnancy, dry up and die, in the name of Jesus. Father Lord, protect my pregnancy forever, in the name of Jesus. Every arrow that was fired at my pregnancy, backfire, in the name of Jesus. You my pregnancy, refuse to be aborted, in the name of Jesus.

THANK YOU!

I'd like to use this time to thank you for purchasing my books and helping my ministry and work. Any copy of my book you buy helps to fund my ministry and family, as well as offering much-needed inspiration to keep writing. My family and I are very thankful, and we take your assistance very seriously.

You have already accomplished so much, but I would appreciate an honest review of some of my books through the link below. This is critical since reviews reflect how much an author's work is respected.

Please visit https://www.amazon.com/review/create-review?asin=B09TDT59M5 or CLICK HERE TO LEAVE A REVIEW

Please be aware that I read and value all comments and reviews. You can always post a review even though you haven't finished the book yet, and then edit your reviews later.

Once again, here is the link:

Please visit https://www.amazon.com/review/create-review?asin=B09TDT59M5 or CLICK HERE TO LEAVE A REVIEW

Thank you so much as you spare a precious moment of your time and may God bless you and meet you at the very point of your need.

You can also send me an email to prayermadu@yahoo.com if you encounter any difficulty while writing your review.

OTHER BOOKS BY PRAYER MADUEKE

1. 100 Days Prayers to Wake Up Your Lazarus
2. 15 Deliverance Steps to Everlasting Life
3. 21/40 Nights of Decrees and Your Enemies Will Surrender
4. 35 Deliverance Steps to Everlasting Rest
5. 35 Special Dangerous Decrees
6. 40 Prayer Giants
7. Alone with God
8. Americans, May I Have Your Attention Please
9. Avoid Academic Defeats
10. Because You Are Living Abroad
11. Biafra of My Dream
12. Breaking Evil Yokes
13. Call to Renew Covenant
14. Command the Morning, Day and Night
15. Community Liberation and Solemn Assembly
16. Comprehensive Deliverance
17. Confront and Conquer Your Enemy
18. Contemporary Politicians' Prayers for Nation Building
19. Crossing the Hurdles
20. Dangerous Decrees to Destroy Your Destroyers (Series)
21. Dealing with Institutional Altars
22. Deliverance by Alpha and Omega

FREE EBOOKS

In order to say a 'Thank You' for purchasing *Prayers for Pregnant Women*, I offer these books to you in appreciation.

> [Click here or go to madueke.com/free-gift to download the eBooks now](madueke.com/free-gift) <

CHRISTIAN COUNSELLING

We were created for a greater purpose than only survival and God wants us to live a full life.

If you need prayer or counselling, or if you have any other inquiries, please visit the counselling page on my website madueke.com/counselling to know when I will be available for a phone call.

EMAIL NEWSLETTER & ANNOUNCEMENTS

Never miss a message from me again! People who read my newsletters say that they have been one of the most important tools in their Christian walk. The best part is that a subscription is, and always will be, completely free. As a subscriber on my mailing list, you'll be the first to hear about my new book releases, be invited to my weekly prayer sessions, and get reminders about my blog posts and other helpful information.

To subscribe, please visit the newsletter page on my website madueke.com/newsletter.

AN INVITATION TO BECOME A MINISTRY PARTNER

In response to several calls from readers of my books on how to collaborate with this ministry, we are grateful to provide our ministry's bank details.

Be assured that our continued prayers for you will be answered according to God's Word, and as you remain faithful by sowing seeds of faith, God will never forget your labors of love in Christ Jesus.

Send your Seeds to:

In Nigeria & Africa

Bank Name: **Access Bank**

Account Name: **Prayer Emancipation Missions**

Account Number: **0692638220**

In the United States & the rest of the World

Bank Name: **Bank of America**

Account Name: **Roseline C. Madueke**

Account Number: **483079070578**

You can also visit the donation page on my website to donate online: www.madueke.com/donate.

www.ingramcontent.com/pod-product-compliance
Lightning Source LLC
Chambersburg PA
CBHW051357150726
48000CB00003B/1231